# THE DANGER OF ANGER

TERYL W. TODD

# THE DANGER OF ANGER

TERYL W. TODD

THE DANGER OF ANGER: *Removing Anger at the Root*

By Teryl W. Todd

Published by Blaze Publishing House
P.O. Box 184
Mansfield, TX 76063
www.blazepublishinghouse.com



Direct quotations from the Bible appear in italic type.

Cover design by David Lunsford and Ryan Forkel. Photograph by istockphoto.com.

Manuscript Development by Kent Booth

Editing and Interior Design by Laura-Lee Booth

Library of Congress Control Number: 2010909858



ISBN 10: 0-9825289-5-7

ISBN-13: 978-0-9825289-5-2

This book is dedicated to my wife, Kathy, and to our children: Terri, Kathryn, and Kristin; and to our son-in-law, Byron Jones.

You are the best!
Thank you for your love and support!

# Acknowledgments

I am indebted to Kent and Laura-Lee Booth of Blaze Publishing House; and to my friend, Dr. Jerry Horner. Without their encouragement and editorial skills, this project would never have come to completion.

Finally, I wish to thank the greatest people in the world—the staff, pastors, deacons, trustees, and congregation at Evangel Assembly of God in Tallahassee, Florida!

# Contents

# INTRODUCTION

I just couldn't figure it out! In my mind, the pieces didn't fit together. How could I enjoy such wonderful, intimate times with God, preach under the anointing of the Holy Spirit, and see numerous people get saved in my ministry . . . but still have anger simmering inside me? I wrestled with feelings I did not understand and asked myself questions like:

*"Why do I feel like I am being overtaken by my emotions?"*

*"What is the source of this awful bitterness that claws at my soul?"*

Several years ago, these were the questions that plagued me on a regular basis. Here I was, the pastor

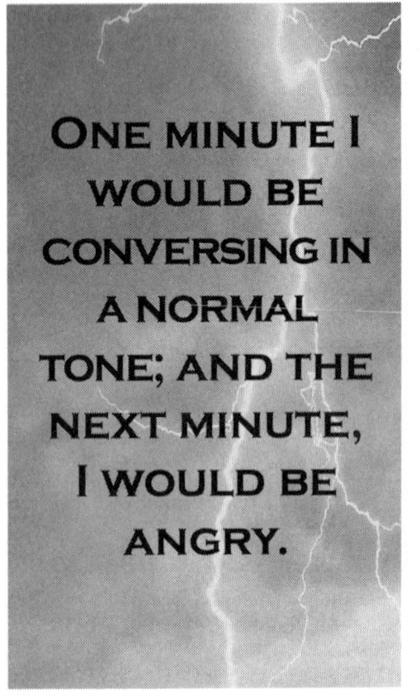


of a great church, heavily involved in ministering to people; yet, I was struggling on the inside. A deep-seated anger was ruling my life and affecting those I loved. To my horror and disgust, I found myself raising my voice at my beautiful wife, Kathy, and at my children and co-workers. One minute I would be conversing in a normal tone; and the next minute, I would be angry. The fuse kept getting shorter and shorter.

When my outbursts became more frequent and more difficult to control, I began to take frightful inventory, thinking:

*"What is wrong with me?"*

I just couldn't figure out why I was acting this way or what was the reason for all this rage. This was one of the very few times—maybe the only time—I have felt at a complete loss.

There was only one thing I knew to do, so I did it.

In desperation, I took my Bible and isolated myself to be alone with God. This is what I always did when I needed to hear from the Lord, and He was always faithful to meet with me. As I fasted and prayed, I cried out:

> *"God, I don't know what's going on inside of me! I've got all this uncontrollable anger and frustration. I'm no longer the master of my emotions. Lord, I repent. Please forgive me!"*

In accordance with the teaching of the Bible concerning the power of agreement, I talked to my wife and my parents. The three of them united in prayer with me and for me. Then, the thought struck me that perhaps this could be a stronghold, such as Paul discusses in 2 Corinthians:

> ***"For the weapons of our warfare are not carnal but mighty in God for pulling down strongholds."***
>
> **2 Corinthians 10:4**

I knew that a stronghold was a system of thoughts empowered by our emotions which are contrary to the Word of God. I had preached about this subject on many occasions and had personally counseled many people on the same topic. So, I began to practice what I had preached and began the process of casting down a spirit and an attitude of anger in the name of Jesus. I made a list of all the scriptures which dealt with emotions—specifically, anger—and meditated on every word. Continuously, I cried out, "God, please help me!"

I was doing everything I knew to do.

After exhausting all of my options and "spiritual fixes," my efforts were futile. I admit, there was some release; but the measure of unresolved frustration still quaked inside me. It was still a mystery. So, I read several books that dealt with anger.

Slowly, in all of the reading and perseverance, I began to learn some things about this nagging problem. But knowledge alone wasn't sufficient to heal my damaged emotions. My breakthrough came when I finally sat down with a counselor. He helped me identify the "points of pain" that were fueling the fire of frustration in my life, and the process of healing began. (Notice the word "process.")

During this entire journey, God has revealed some remarkable truths which have helped to set me free; and I believe they will also bring answers, hope, and deliverance to others.

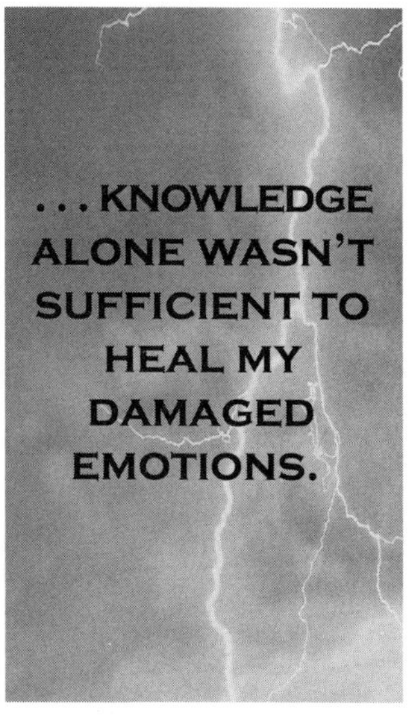


If you have dealt with anger issues in the past or are dealing with them now, I believe this will be one of the most important books you may ever read. If you are seeking answers to why you feel the way you do—the anger, the rage, the despair—let me assure you that you are not alone. I know. I have been there! But, I also know there is an answer that brings freedom.

I can assure you that if you respond to the following pages in faith and not fear, obedience and not shame, the Spirit of God is going to set you free. You will experience not a temporary "fix," but a lifetime of freedom! *The Danger of Anger* is a journey—mainly, my journey—which leads down a path to healing, restoration, and freedom from anger.

Let's take this journey . . . together.

# ROBERT'S STORY

Everyone was certain that Robert would make it to the top. He was blessed with all the accoutrements of success. He was handsome and intelligent; and above all, the young attorney possessed extraordinary people skills. He made rapid advancements in the political arena, and officials in high places began to take notice. No one was surprised when Robert was asked to serve as a special advisor to the king. Time and time again, Robert's wisdom and counsel brought solutions that won praise from other cabinet members. "Having him here is like God speaking directly to us," they would say. And the king agreed.

Robert's life was good.

In addition to making tremendous headway in his political career, Robert was progressing in his family life. God had blessed him with a wonderful wife, handsome sons, and striking daughters. As the years passed, his children married and gave him many beautiful grandchildren, including one granddaughter who particularly grabbed Robert's heart. Every evening, this little girl would crawl up on her granddaddy's lap just to laugh and hear another story. Weekends and holidays were filled with special moments as their relationship grew ever closer.

This granddaughter grew up to be a stunningly beautiful woman, able to pick any man she desired for her husband. But she was particular, and she was determined to wait for the perfect one. Finally, he came along, but he was considerably older than she was. He was a decorated military hero, still actively serving his country. Finally, the wait was over. Robert's favorite granddaughter was now a loving and committed wife, and he could not have been happier!

As usual in military life, there are frequent periods of separation between husband and wife. This reality was something the newlywed couple had anticipated, but being apart brought its own set of challenges. Because duty had called, Robert's grandson-in-law was stationed in a war-ridden hotspot several hundred miles away from his bride. It was during this time that Robert and his wife first began hearing rumors; the substance of which was that their beloved granddaughter had done the unthinkable. The whispered reports declared that she was having an affair with another man—but not just any man. In fact, it was with the person whom Robert had honored with many years of distinguished service—the king.

Robert was overwhelmed with a gamut of emotions, foremost of which was sadness over betrayal and broken trust. The same man, whom he had pledged to give his life for, was now destroying his own family. As Robert tried to muster up the courage to confront both of them, the story became even more sinister. His granddaughter was pregnant by the king. Robert began to question how such a thing could be. Why would this man, who already had multiple wives and possessed the power to have any woman he wanted, go after someone less than half his age, let alone his granddaughter? There were no satisfactory answers to his frenzied questions.

Robert agonized over the dilemma of how the two lovers would explain their sinful actions to his granddaughter's military husband. After all, he was away defending the very king who was deceiving him. The king, however, had devised a devilish scheme that would render an explanation unnecessary. In flagrant and vicious abuse of his power, he arranged to have his lover's husband killed on the enemy's front lines. Robert's nightmare continued, as did his questions. He just couldn't understand why his boss had to ruin his granddaughter's life and bring shame on the family. His heart burned with indignation and anger. But Robert, a patient and wise man, suppressed his resentment until the appropriate time.

And that time did indeed come.

Many years passed, and another scandal tarnished the monarchy, creating a media firestorm. Every news agency and tabloid published headlines that proclaimed, "King's Son Rapes Half-Sister." Even with overwhelming evidence, the king blatantly denied the charges and refused to deal with the situation. His apathetic attitude infuriated the people; but more importantly, it fueled an outrage within his own household. Another son, irate at his father's indifference, took matters into his own hands by killing his half-brother who had raped his sister. To escape certain death for his act of vengeance, this young man fled to a neighboring country, where he received asylum.

After many years, the exiled son returned home. During the time of the son's absence, Robert's hostility had escalated into a deep-rooted seed of bitterness. Recognizing his opportunity for revenge, he began meeting with the former fugitive. Although they were supposedly mentoring sessions, their meetings were actually part of a conspiracy. Robert planted seeds of rebellion in the young man's heart. He asked, "Do you know that you can become our king? It's easy. Just become friends with the military leaders, and they will help you dethrone your father!"

The evil-seeded suggestions always included vain flattery. "Our country really needs someone who is strong, young, courageous, and who carries the king's name. That person is you!"

It didn't take long for Robert's suggestions to

take root. The once-disgraced son won the allegiance of the military leaders and successfully deposed his father and all of his administration from power. And it was no surprise that Robert became the new king's chief advisor. Everything was restored, with the government functioning smoothly; and as long as the new king followed Robert's advice, all went well. Things were rolling along just fine, until one day . . .

Robert persuaded the new king that it would be in the best interest of the new regime to send a commando squad to murder his father. It made sense. His father's death would guarantee that the former ruler would never recapture the capitol. Robert intended his advice to be more than a safety precaution. For him, it meant that his long-awaited vindication was just one command away. The assassination of the man who had violated his granddaughter would bring justice. However, Robert's plan suffered

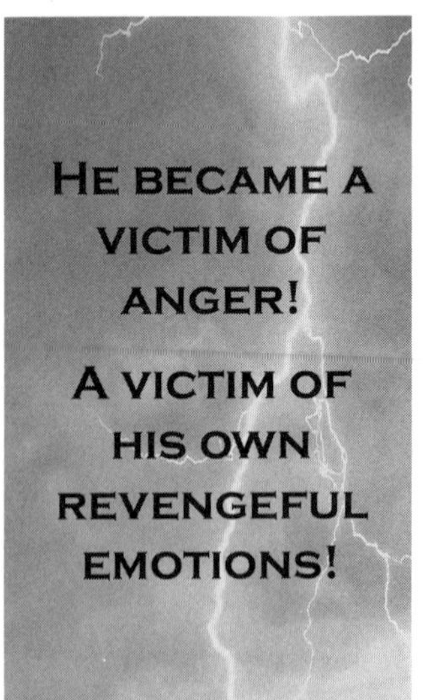

a bitter disappointment when the new king refused to follow his advice. Robert could see the writing on the wall—the old king would regain power, and his own life was about to end in tragedy.

You can read this entire story, including its outcome, in the Book of Second Samuel.

You see, this is not the story of a man named Robert and some obscure king, but rather a man named Ahithophel and a king named . . . David! Ahithophel's precious granddaughter was Bathsheba, the woman who will be forever marked as having committed adultery with David. And how did Ahithophel deal with his unresolved anger and frustration? The Bible tells us:

> ***"Now when Ahithophel saw that his advice was not followed, he saddled a donkey, and arose and went home to his house, to his city. Then he put his household in order, and hanged himself, and died; and he was buried in his father's tomb."***
>
> **2 Samuel 17:23**

What a tragedy! If you put that story in today's

vernacular, it would read something like this:

> "When Ahithophel saw that his advice was not followed, he got into his Porsche®, and drove to his hometown. First, he stopped by his lawyer's office, then he dropped in on his accountant. Lastly, he visited his insurance broker. After he made sure all of his personal affairs were in order, he went out and committed suicide. The next day, he was buried."
>
> The end.

What a bitter and tragic ending. Ahithophel fell prey to a life-threatening disease—not cancer or heart disease or even AIDS. He became a victim of anger! A victim of his own revengeful emotions!

## DISCUSSION QUESTIONS

1. Ahithophel and his family felt controlled by someone, and they could do absolutely nothing about it. Can you relate to the emotion that builds when you realize someone else is calling the shots and you can do little to get back into the driver's seat?

2. How do you cope when feeling this kind of "helplessness?"

   (a) How do you respond when people place unreasonable demands on you?

3. No human was created to be controlled by another. As school children, we are taught that freedom is a gift to be cherished. Yet, at the whim of King David, Bathsheba's marriage was violated and her husband was killed. Can you share a time when you felt controlled by something or someone?

4. Can you relate to any of the following statements? Which ones and why?

    - "When I grew up I was expected to obey the rules with no questions asked."

    - "When I share my opinion or preference, I am often putdown or made to feel like my views are unimportant."

    - "No one is willing to talk with me about my feelings and perceptions, and I feel controlled."

    - "I often feel that my performance is all that matters to others."

    - "I would like to speak more freely about personal matters, but to do so would only lead to arguments or disappointments."

- "I feel like I live in the middle of a bunch of critics."

# GET TO THE ROOT

For many years, every time I read the story of Ahithophel, I found myself asking questions like:

"Why did it have to end that way?"

"What went wrong?"

"Where was the disconnect?"

What I have come to understand is something of the despair and anguish that tormented him. There have been times in my life that I, too had felt like I was a pawn, the puppet of someone else. But mere identification with these emotions was not producing

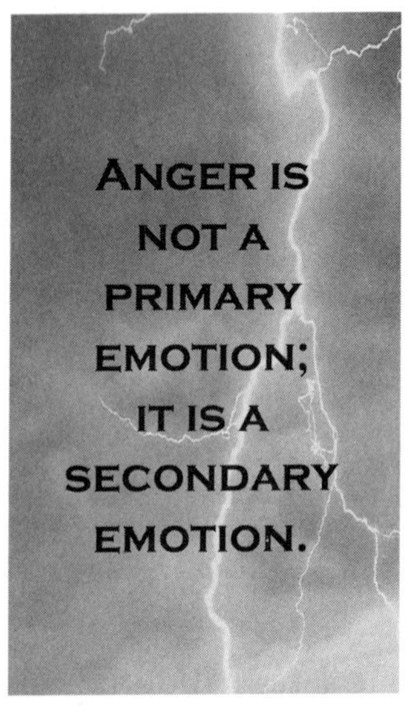


any answers. I had to go back to the root of the problem and ask the question: "Where does anger come from?"

The answer was the first step in my victory over the emotion that had so adversely affected my life. Honestly, I was surprised at first, but the more I studied and prayed, the more freedom came to my soul. The truth is that God created us all in His likeness and image. God created every part of us, *including our emotions.* It's easy to understand why God would give us emotions like joy, trust, surprise, and anticipation. Those don't seem to be the "bad" ones. But anger is an emotion, too, just like all the others that God placed in us. Anger exists by divine design; we just have to learn how to manage it properly.

There are two different views of anger in the New Testament. The first one is found in Paul's letter to the Ephesians:

***"Be angry, and do not sin: do not let the sun go down on your wrath."***

**Ephesians 4:26**

Clearly, the Apostle Paul is saying that it is possible to be angry without being in sin. But, take a look at what James has to say:

***"So then, my beloved brethren, let every man be swift to hear, slow to speak, slow to wrath; for the wrath of man does not produce the righteousness of God."***

**James 1:19-20**

Initially, these two passages almost sound contradictory to each other! Paul is saying that it's okay to be angry . . . just don't sin. On the other hand, James tells us that anger is unrighteousness. Which one is right?

They both are!

One of the most important truths to learn about

anger is that anger is not a primary emotion; it is a secondary emotion. In other words, anger is not the root problem. It's an impulsive reaction. When things don't go our way, we *react* with anger. If someone has done something wrong to us, then we get angry. Anger is the reaction; "things" act as triggers, causing anger to rear its ugly head. Therefore, to understand how to deal with the secondary emotion of anger, we must first examine some of the root issues that can trigger it and set it into motion.

## TRIGGER #1 - THE KISS OF DEATH

Look back at Ahithophel's story. His anger and despair started when David and his granddaughter, Bathsheba, entered into an adulterous affair. It was a reaction to something that caught him totally off guard and shocked him alarmingly. What was it that made him react this way? I call it "the kiss of death."

Betrayal.

Betrayal is one of the most powerful tools of the enemy. Why? Because it's more than just anyone letting you down. It's being disappointed by someone who is very close to you. Husband. Wife. A member of the immediate family. A close relative. A trusted friend. An employee or employer. A spiritual leader. Betrayal is a fatal strike to the heart, a sucker-punch to your emotions. The "kiss of death" leaves a deep wound with open, exposed gashes in the soul.

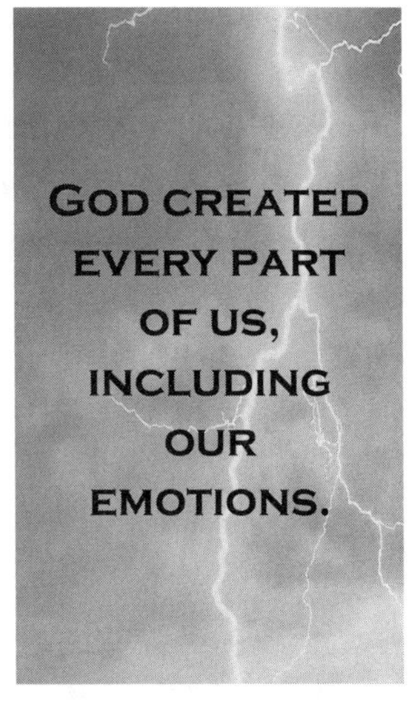


If you have never suffered betrayal by someone close to you, it just means that you haven't lived long enough! I assure you, that day will come. It did for me, and I wasn't ready for it. Sometimes in ministry, the people who I helped the most, turned against me. Why? I'm not altogether sure. Some would be nice to my face, but critical behind my back. Betrayal hurts!

At times, I questioned if anyone else had ever had such an experience. In fact, many have, including King David, as he described it in Psalm 55:

> ***"For it is not an enemy who reproaches me; then I could bear it. Nor is it one who hates me who has exalted himself against me; then I could hide from him. But it was you, a man my equal, my companion and my acquaintance. We took sweet counsel together, and walked to the house of God in the throng."***
>
> **Psalm 55:12-14**

David expresses it very plainly. Your enemies are not the ones who will betray you; they couldn't even if they tried! They don't have the ability to. Why? Because under most circumstances, you don't make yourself vulnerable to your enemies. But, those you love, admire, respect, and with whom you feel a close relationship—*those* are the ones who have the ability to betray you. How many times have you been driving down the highway and someone you didn't even know gave you an obscene gesture? Did it wreck your day? Probably not. In fact, it might have made you laugh. But, if someone you truly love and admire talks bad about you behind your back, steals from you, or cheats you, it feels like someone knocked the wind right out of your sails.

Friend, sometimes people in whom you've invested your time, energy, money, guidance, love, care, and grace will turn on you! It's a part of life. Before you get totally wrecked, remember this one thing: you're not the only person who has ever experienced betrayal.

Jesus did.

He was betrayed by two of His closest disciples: Peter and Judas. Peter denied Him three times, but later repented and was restored. Judas was also one of Jesus' closest friends and disciples; yet, he sold out the Messiah for a measly payout of 30 pieces of silver. In the Garden of Gethsemane, he identified Jesus by kissing Him on the cheek. In reality, it was the first "kiss of death." Jesus' fate was sealed, and Judas' job was complete. But he couldn't bear the guilt of what he had done. Overtaken by remorse, Judas tried to return the money and, just like Ahithophel, took his own life.

## TRIGGER #2 - A LIFE OUT OF CONTROL

Let's face it. Almost everybody at one time or another feels their life is out of control. It's like we are flying down life's highway with the cruise control stuck at 120 miles-per-hour . . . with no brakes! I've driven down that road. It's when we attempt to regain some control that anger can surface. And, it seems that the more out of control we are, the angrier we become. But, there is an explanation for this reaction.

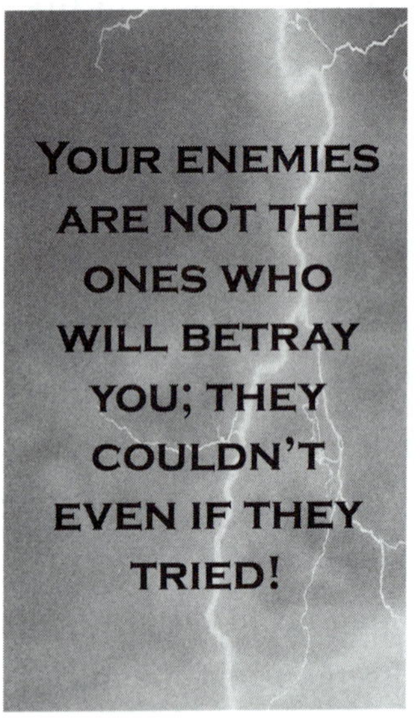


Many times, angry people are simply trying to communicate their inside hurts to the outside world. For some, it's the only way they know how to reach out for attention. In these cases, anger manifests itself in different ways: fits of rage, yelling, intense emotions, and high levels of irritation. It's all a cry for somebody to take notice, to understand what they are going through, and to offer sympathy and assistance.

If only it were that simple.

You see, most people don't know how to react to

someone who is angry, especially if it involves confrontation. The majority of society avoids *any* type of confrontation like it's the plague! Instead of facing a potential altercation with an angry person, they choose the absolute worse alternative—to ignore them completely. The theory is that if you just leave it alone, it will fix itself. No, it won't. Now, there's a person who is crying out for someone—anyone—to listen to and relate to their hurt, but no one wants to take the risk of listening. So, the anger keeps building and intensifying.

It reminds me of the old saying, "If mamma ain't happy, ain't *nobody* happy!" This saying may be true as it is, but if you want to make mamma *really* mad, just ignore her the next time when she's angry. That will send her through the roof! But the solution is easy. Just ask her, "Mamma, are you okay? What's going on inside of you? Are you sure you're alright?" This type of concern and care acts like a pressure release valve that drains out all the pain and resentment. It gets past the anger and to the root of the problem—the feeling of being overwhelmed and out of control.

## TRIGGER #3 - GOALS OUT OF REACH

I remember reading about a man who had an extremely frustrating week at work. On Friday afternoon, he decided to do something that would surely help vent some of his frustration. Mow the grass! After changing into his old work clothes, he went to the garage and prepared to achieve his goal. The grass was high, the lawnmower was full of gas; the perfect way to release his pent-up frustration. Everything was going according to plan . . . until he pulled the starter cable. Nothing. He pulled it again. Nothing. He thought, "Well, maybe the engine just needs a little priming." So, he kept pulling and pulling and pulling, each time with more vigor. Still, nothing. Every unsuccessful pull produced more and more anger. His wife and two kids were nearby, but their oblivious unconcern only added to his frustration. Still, he pulled and pulled and pulled with the same results . . .

Nothing.

His plan to relieve his tension was not only failing; it was actually making the situation worse! So, he reverted to what seemed to be the only solution fitting for the occasion. He stormed into his house, grabbed his 12-gauge shotgun, walked back outside, and filled the lawnmower full of holes! Killed it dead!

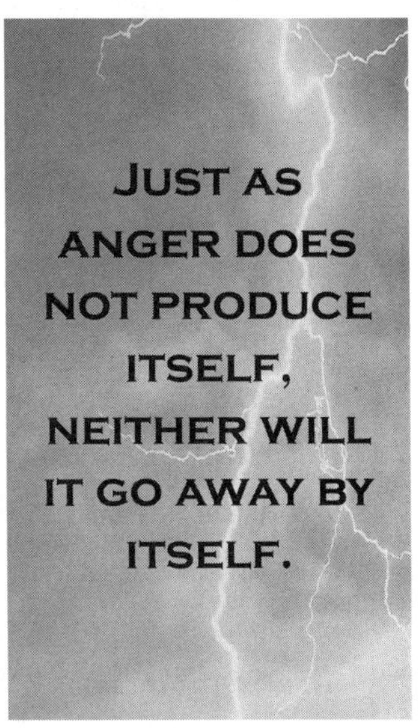


Establishing goals that are out of reach or failing to reach those that are attainable can be extremely frustrating. We get angry when we think there's something or someone keeping us from getting to where we want to go. Now, you're probably not going to resolve your frustrations like the man and his lawn mower, but anger can sure make you feel that way!

## LOOK PAST THE SURFACE

Betrayal, a life out of control, and goals out of reach are some of the most common triggers that produce anger, but they are far from being the only ones. Feeling hurt, disrespected, rejected, and violated can also be root causes which produce the fruit of anger. Just as anger does not produce itself, neither will it go away by itself.

## DISCUSSION QUESTIONS

1. Anger is an emotion that is common to every person. We are imperfect people living in an imperfect world, and we frequently encounter this emotion. The word "anger" is used to describe a number of terms, including: frustration, irritability, annoyance, blowing off steam, and fretting. Do you experience any of these things on a regular basis? Which ones?

2. Can you identify the underlying reasons for your anger?

3. Anger has many faces. It can manifest as impatience, a critical attitude, shutting down and withdrawing from someone, inward annoyance, feeling overwhelmed, worry, fear, discouragement that makes you want to quit, aggression, blaming others, being defensive, frustrated, sarcastic, speaking too sternly, being depressed, and adopting an "I don't care attitude." How

frequently do you experience these kinds of feelings?

4. Have you experienced:

    - Betrayal?
    - A life out of control?
    - Goals out of reach?

    (a) How do you respond to these things?

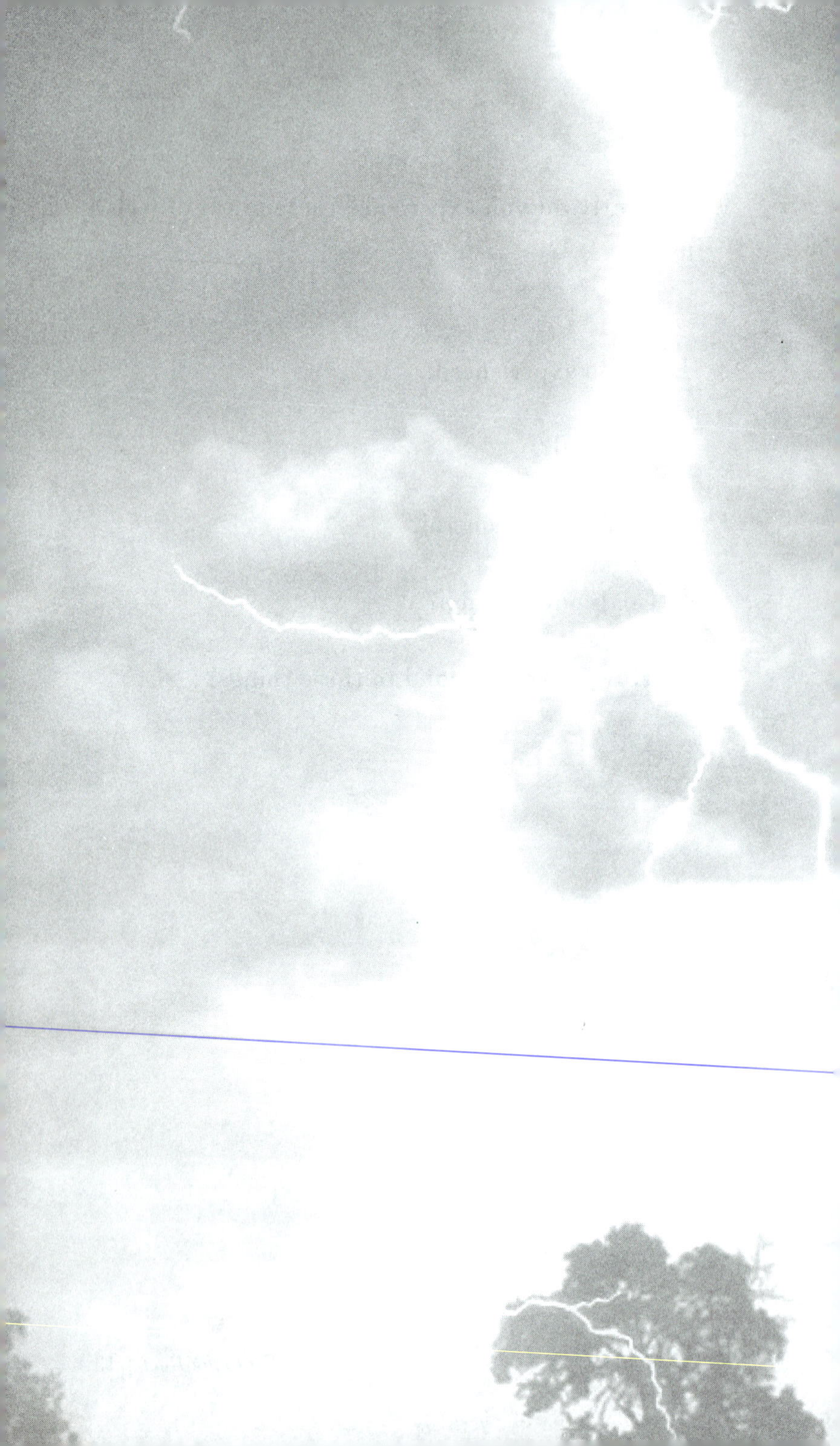

# DEALING WITH EMOTIONAL PAIN

My roots were deep. I didn't even realize that some of them existed. I tried everything in my power to rid myself of the annoyance lurking beneath the surface of my soul but to no avail. As a pastor, I spent countless hours studying my Bible and researching the subject of anger, but something was still missing in my life. Even though my knowledge was increasing, the residue of anger and frustration inside me would not dissipate. Eventually, I came to the conclusion that the remedy was beyond my reach, and I needed to talk to other pastors and counselors for advice and help. It just seemed like the logical thing to do.

One counselor told me, "Teryl, what you need to

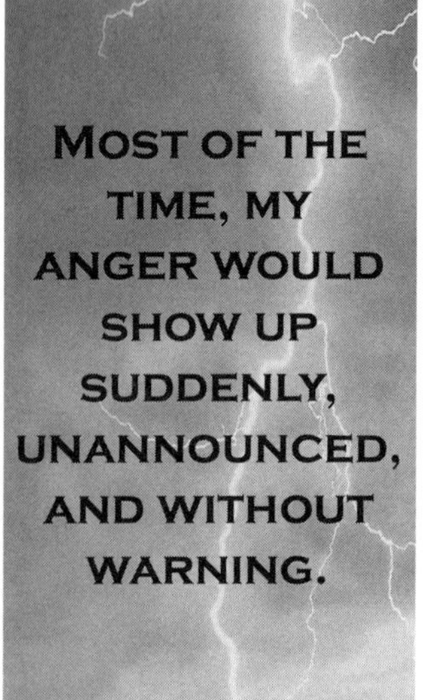


do is exercise every day and get some of that aggression out." It sounded reasonable, so I began lifting weights and running several miles a day. Six months passed, and I was in pretty good physical shape . . . but I was still angry.

Another counselor said, "Anytime you feel anger welling up in you, take a tennis ball and throw it as hard as you can against a brick wall. Do it until you can't do it anymore!" I took his advice, but there were still no results.

One pastor suggested I take up a hobby like refinishing furniture. It sounded reasonable, so I turned part of the basement of our home into a workshop. I made all kinds of things down there. It wasn't long before I became an expert at making gold leaf picture frames. In time, there wasn't a square inch on any wall in our house that wasn't covered with a picture! The experience of learning a new hobby was great (and my wife loved not having to buy any new picture frames), but I was still struggling with antagonistic feelings.

Nothing seemed to work. To make things worse, the guilt I felt of being a minister of the Gospel, yet wrestling to keep a lid on my rage, zapped me of all emotional energy. Most of the time, my anger would show up suddenly, unannounced, and without warning. I began to ask myself, "Why can't I control these feelings?" After all of the so-called "fixes" failed, I really began to think I was going to battle these feelings for the rest of my life. I was at my wit's end, and desperation was quickly overtaking me.

And then came help—real help!

## THE QUESTION NO ONE ASKED

I went to see a Christian counselor who eventually became a dear friend. I will never forget the first time I went to see him. I said, "I've got all this anger in me, and I don't know what to do. Other counselors and pastors suggested several things to help, but nothing has worked. Please, help me."

This man leaned towards me and asked something that *none* of the others had asked. He asked me, "Teryl, what's the Holy Spirit saying to you?" I was astonished by his question, but even more startling was the fact that I could not give him an answer. In my entire search for help, I had not taken the time to stop and listen to the voice of the Holy Spirit. Downcast with embarrassment, I replied, "I don't know; I'm not hearing Him." The counselor graciously answered, "Well, let's just see what Jesus has to say about what's going on inside you."

You would think that as a pastor, I would be very eager to follow this word of advice and dive headfirst into the words of Jesus! Quite honestly, I wasn't all that excited about it. You see, I was brought up to believe that introspection and soul-searching was only for women; a *real* man should be strong enough to handle his own business. Men shouldn't have to reach inside and "connect" to their inner self. After all, isn't it true that men are rocks, pillars of strength, and they are not supposed to cry?

Was I ever wrong!

As I began to pray—and for the first time ask the Holy Spirit, "What's going on inside me?"—the Spirit of God began to speak very clearly. He said, "There are things in your life that you have not grieved over. You've got emotional pain." And He was right. The truth of the matter was that I had an enormous amount of pain down in my soul. But, instead of dealing with it, I did what multitudes of other people do—I lived in complete denial.

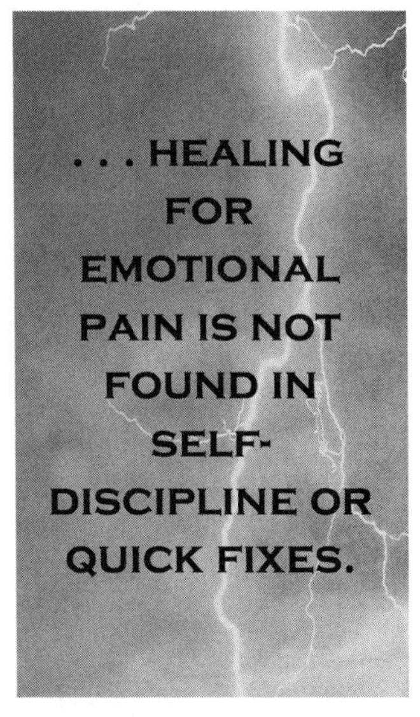


What I didn't realize was that the pains were *not* going away.

## SUPPRESSION

The opening line of the Bill Withers' classic, *Lean on Me*, says, "Sometimes in our lives, we all have pain; we all have sorrow." Mr. Withers was right! Everyone deals with negative experiences. Like betrayal, it's a part of life. However, the way we respond to these hurts defines our future. One of the most common ways—and the most dangerous—is to deny that the incident or hurt ever occurred.

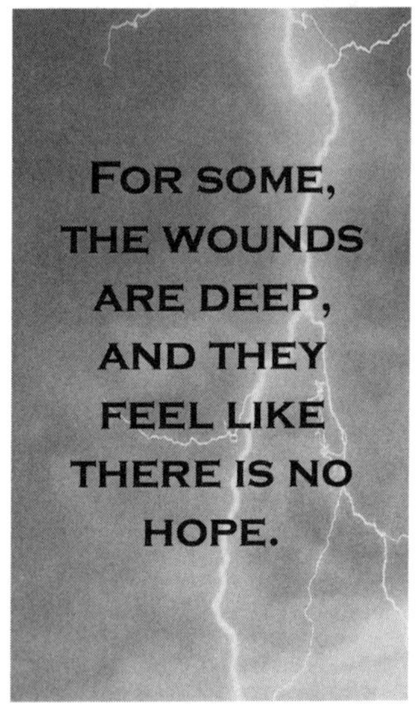


For example, during childhood, many children suffer emotional hurt. The problem is that youngsters aren't equipped to process emotional pain, so they unconsciously push these feelings down inside them. For a season, they repress the pain and the memories. They live and act as if the event never happened. Year after year, they continue to repress and ignore these feelings. But, eventually, the passing of time or some circumstance will trigger the release of these emotions. Sometimes, "out of nowhere," strong feelings can come to the surface under the guise of anger and rage.

**STUCK!**

While some people try to ignore emotional pain, others feel like they are stuck with it for the rest of their lives. Before seeing this counselor, that was what I thought—but it was a trap. Actually, it's an outright lie from the enemy! When we begin to realize how God designed us, then we can see the truth and be set free.

The Bible says that God created us as a three-part being—spirit, soul, and body (1 Thessalonians 5:23). Our soul is the resting place for our thoughts, will, and emotions. (Remember, anger is an *emotion.*) Our soul is not only the part of us that processes information and interacts in this world; it's also the place that carries our emotional pain. When we were born again, our *spirit* man became brand new, BUT our soul and body remained the same. This is why even Christians can still have struggles with negative feelings. The root of emotional hurt that was planted in their soul before they were born again is still there. But there is good news!

No one has to stay stuck there.

The Bible says we can be free from past hurts by

the "renewing of our mind" (Romans 12:2). That, my friend, is a process. It doesn't happen overnight, but it can happen. Sadly, some people never understand how to renew their minds, and the result is: they stay stuck in their pain and live with anger, rage, and frustration during their entire Christian life. For some, the wounds are deep, and they feel like there is no hope. But God promises all the hope they need in the simple declaration:

> **"My grace is sufficient for you, for My strength is made perfect in weakness."**
>
> **2 Corinthians 12:9**

All the heavy weights I triumphantly pressed, all the exhausting miles I sprinted and walked and limped, all the tennis balls I defiantly hurled, and all the picture frames I tediously crafted failed to remedy my problem. I finally learned that healing for emotional pain is not found in self-discipline or quick fixes. Only when I cried out to God did the Holy Spirit meet me where I was and begin the process of healing my soul. His grace is sufficient for me! That first step to healing can be yours, too. Just say, "Jesus, I'm tired of living this way. I want to get unstuck! I want to be on the pathway to freedom."

You're now ready.

Ready for the process to begin!

## DISCUSSION QUESTIONS

1. Pride is the emotion of self-absorption. It is being preoccupied with ourselves. It is more than just arrogance or conceit; it is at the core of every unhealthy and unproductive emotion and behavior. At the root, pride thinks, "The world and people should be what I say they should be." Why does our pride keep us from acknowledging that we have emotional pain?

2. The opposite of pride is humility. True humility is a choice. A choice not to be self-preoccupied and a choice to acknowledge personal limitations. Why is God's grace reserved only for those who acknowledge their need?

3. Physical exercise and refinishing furniture are both great hobbies, and can get our mind off our problems, however, why do hobbies not rid us of negative emotions?

4. Have you ever asked the Holy Spirit, "What is going-on inside me? What is the source of my anger?" Get quiet and listen for His still, small voice. Then, find a trusted Christian friend or counselor who you can talk with about what is going on inside you.

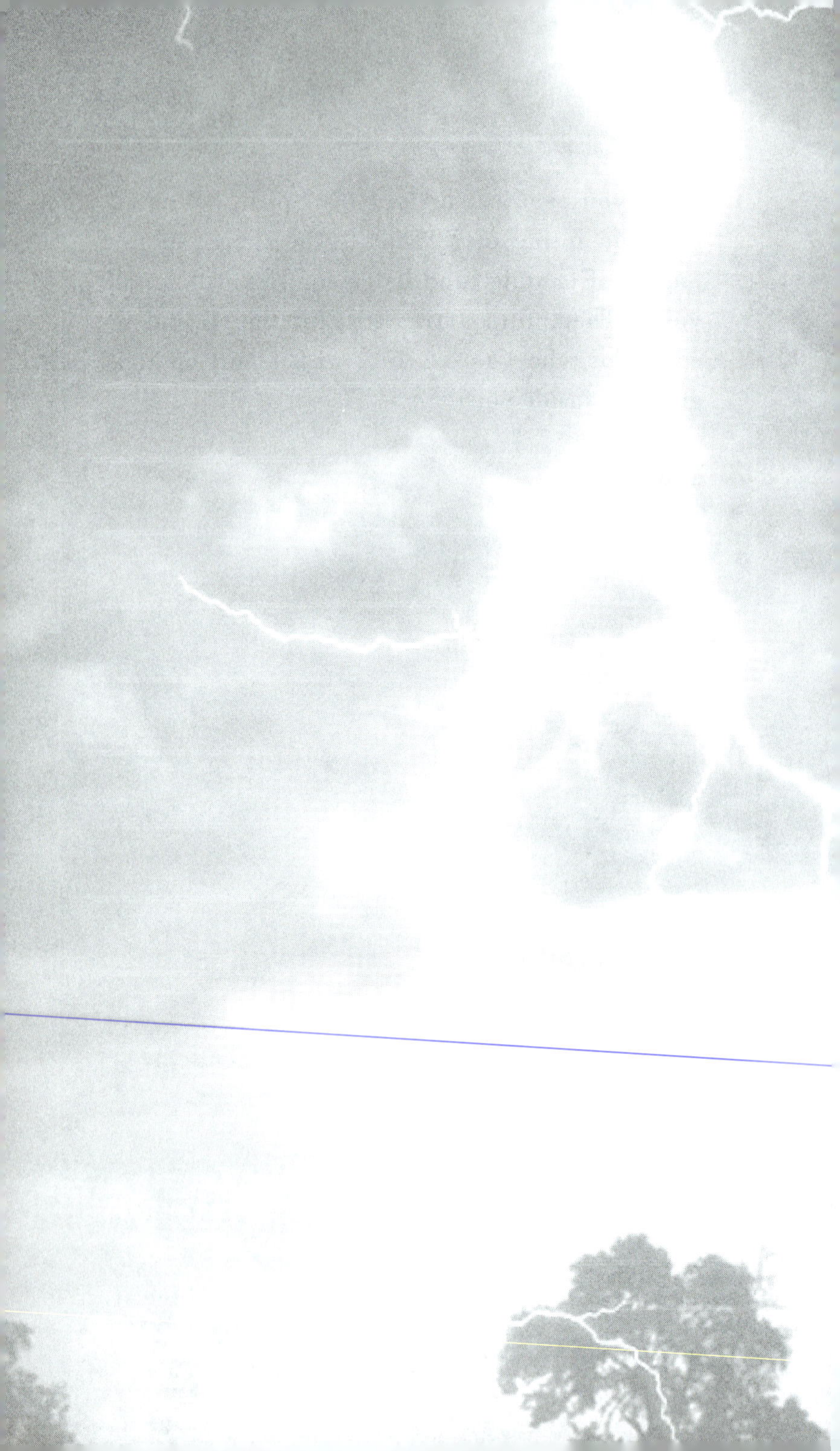

# THE HARDEST EXERCISE OF ALL

Lifting weights was grueling. Running mile after mile was draining. All of the physical exercises to which I subjected my body in an effort to vanquish my anger were arduous. But they all weakened in comparison to what I experienced through the discipline of the Holy Spirit. This *spiritual* exercise would work me to the very core of my soul. It actually required more effort than lifting weights, running, or throwing tennis balls against the wall. My new exercise was wrapped up in one single word:

Forgiveness!

Not just partial forgiveness, but *total* forgiveness. I was about to learn the difference between the two.

## LEARNING THE DIFFERENCES

Partial forgiveness, which most people mistake as total forgiveness, is the attitude that says, "I forgive you; and as long as I don't have to see you again, I'll be fine." Basically, it's an "out of sight, out of mind" mentality. It makes us feel good, like we have done our deed; but in reality, it's no more than lip service. The real indicator of "surface" forgiveness is that we usually want those who injured us to suffer for what they did. We forgive with our words; but in our heart, we believe they should pay a penalty for their words and actions.

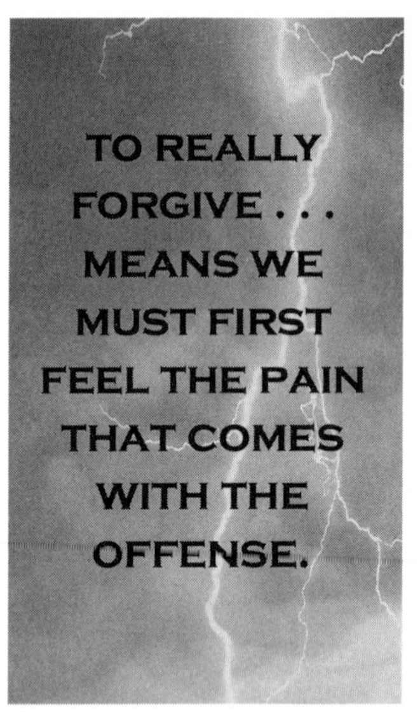


Over the years, I truly believed I had forgiven those who had hurt me. Yet, this underlying thought was tucked away in the back of my mind: "Those who have wronged me are going to reap what they have sown. So, God, make them pay for what they've done to me!" I was only seeing God as my avenger who was going to right the wrongs and take them out! The only problem with this whole line of thinking is that it isn't real forgiveness.

True forgiveness goes much deeper.

To forgive others for a wrong done to you involves more than you simply saying, "I forgive you for what you have done." It also means pardoning the penalty you have placed on them for their actions. Instead of wanting them to experience the pain from their wrongdoing, you tear up the emotional IOU and absorb the cost of the pain yourself. *That's the mark of complete forgiveness.*

Of course, to really forgive someone and cancel the wrong means we must first feel the pain that comes with the offense. In my case, I didn't let myself feel that hurt. Remember, I was a "man's man," and the last thing I ever wanted to do was to grieve and mourn over things that others did to me. I thought, "I can handle it. I've got a lot of stuff to do and little time to get it done. No time to waste crying in my soup or navel-gazing! That's for the weak-minded." Taking the time to stop and analyze my feelings was just not part of my emotional makeup. But little did I realize that this attitude was my main hindrance from walking in total forgiveness. I was dying on the inside without ever knowing it.

Then, I saw true forgiveness in action.

## MORE THAN WORDS

To learn how to forgive completely, we must look at Jesus, the ultimate example. In Matthew chapter 18, Jesus tells the story of a king who not only forgave his subject, but also cancelled a huge debt that the servant owed. In a moment, he wiped away a debt of millions of dollars as though it never existed. Now, *that's* full forgiveness!

It's not just saying, "I forgive you," but actually counting the cost, feeling the pain of what's been done, and then saying, "I'm going to cancel what you owe! You are completely released!"

Just like Jesus did on the cross.

Jesus did more than forgive our sins; He also paid the penalty for our sins! You see, if real forgiveness is merely saying, "I forgive you," then Jesus would have accomplished our forgiveness when He said, "Father, forgive them." If words were enough, He wouldn't have had to suffer death by crucifixion and be resurrected three days later. But for real forgiveness to occur, *words must be accompanied by actions*.

Matthew also records that Jesus cried out, "My God, my God why have you forsaken me?" At this precise moment, Jesus was tearing up God's IOU note! He was taking our place and paying our price for sin. You and I deserve death and hell, but Jesus' actions said, "I am going to become sin in the flesh, so that you can become the righteousness of God!" Not only was this deed true forgiveness in action, but it is also the pattern for you and me to practice. Most of the time, it's not an easy exercise.

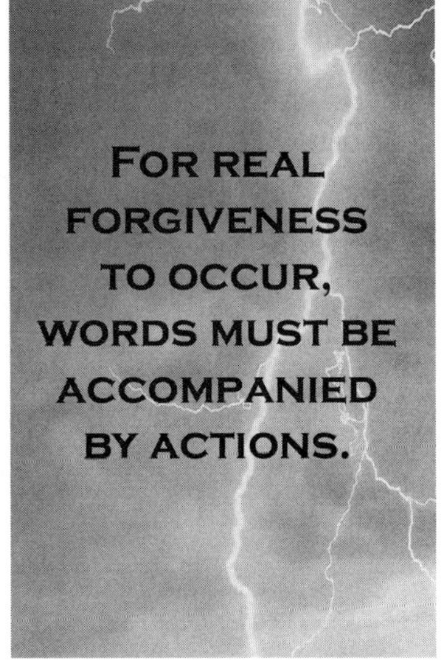


As Christians, we should preset our will to forgive with both our words and actions. As I have already stated, getting hurt and disappointed in life is inevitable. When it happens, the most important thing is the way we respond. When we are determined to walk in forgiveness, these words come out of our spirit:

> *"Lord, I am hurt on the inside. Come and heal my heart. I receive the grace to forgive those who hurt me. Just like Jesus completely forgave me, I release and tear-up any debt I think they owe me. I forgive in Jesus' name."*

However, the alternative—choosing not to forgive—will strongly affect your life.

Harboring anger and unforgiveness is damaging—not to the people who harmed you, but to you!

Refusing to forgive keeps you from being everything God created you to be. Those who hurt you might not even realize their wrong and keep right on living as if nothing happened. But, as long as the offense lingers and festers in your heart, your relationship with God will be hindered in practically every area. Complete forgiveness is the key to complete freedom!

And think about this for a moment: Betrayal

and hurts might even turn out to have a beneficial effect. (I know you're probably scratching your head right now!) Remember Judas? He betrayed the One who loved him dearly. But what was the end result? That one act did something far more significant than merely to identify Jesus to the soldiers; it released Him to "drink from the cup" which was God's will for Him. The cross was Jesus' destiny, and what set the plan into motion was none other than Judas' kiss of death.

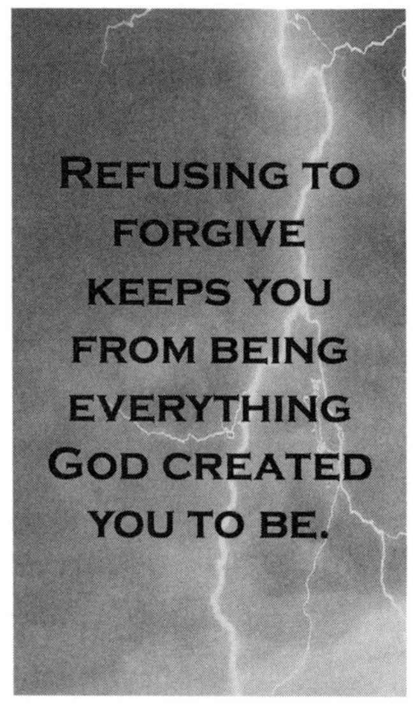


What if Jesus had not completely forgiven Judas for his actions? The answer is obvious. His mission on earth would have been short-changed . . .

. . . And so would have ours.

## DISCUSSION QUESTIONS

1. Can you identify the biggest hurt and disappointment you have ever experienced?

   (a) How did you respond?

   (b) How did you process the pain?

2. What is the difference between partial forgiveness and total forgiveness?

3. What keeps people from totally forgiving others?

4. Have you ever known a Christian who repressed his/her hurts to the point that they had trouble identifying their need to forgive others?

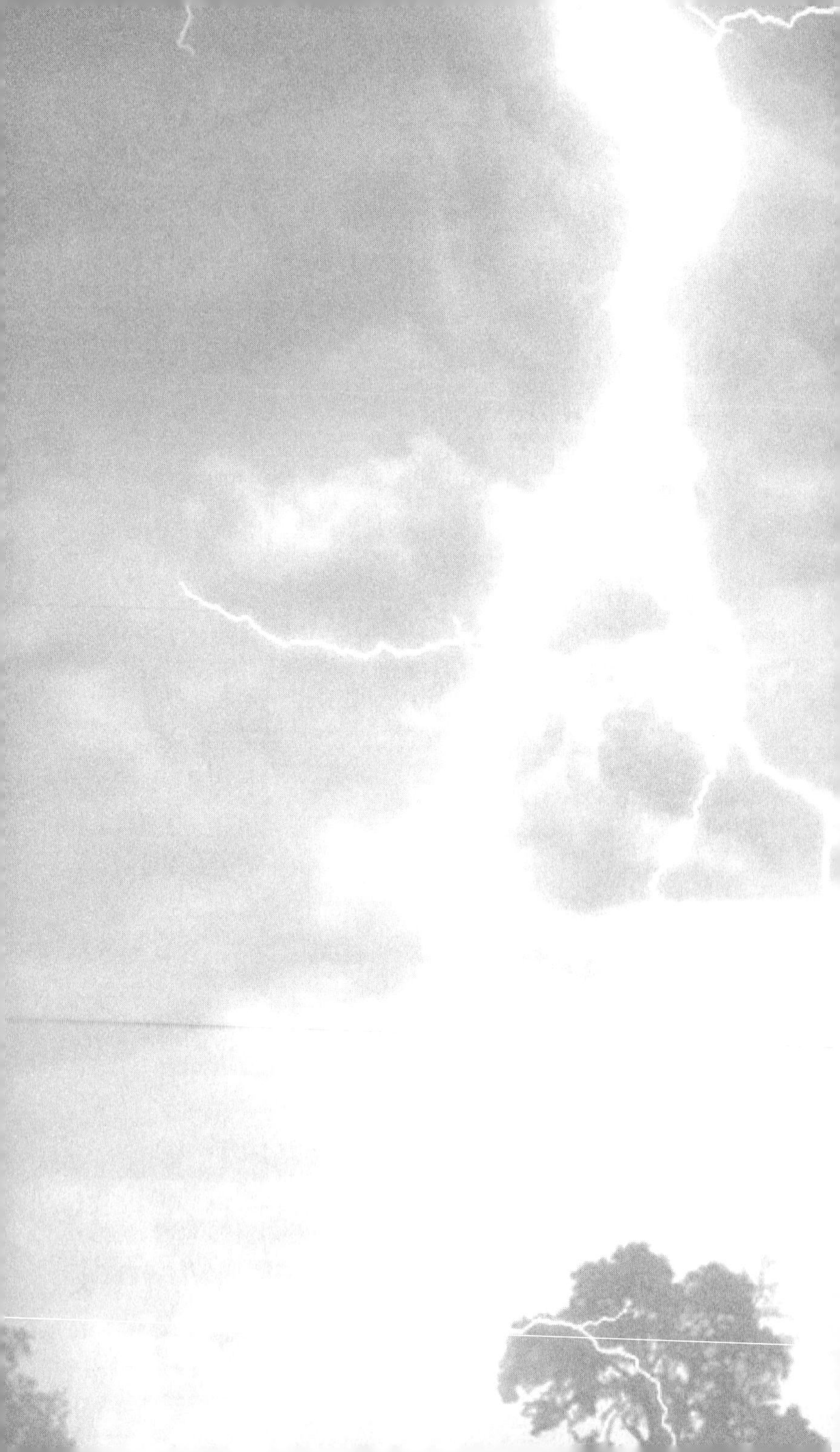

# THE EFFECTS OF UNFORGIVENESS

Full forgiveness is a difficult task. It's a process which demands total commitment. Identifying the sources of hurt and getting them out of our heart can be painful. But, an honest look at the negative effects of anger and unforgiveness provides motivation to start and continue the process.

Let's take a look at a few areas of our lives which are directly affected.

## UNFORGIVENESS LIMITS OUR FAITH

An unforgiving spirit is one of the major hindrances to faith. The Book of Hebrews declares that without

faith, pleasing God is impossible! (Hebrews 11:6) Surely every Christian's goal is to please God, but faith is necessary to accomplish that goal. In Mark chapter 11, Jesus was teaching His disciples about having such faith that they could speak to mountains and command them to move. Furthermore, faith would enable them to have whatever they desired in prayer. How exciting to know the power of prayer and faith! But Jesus taught that there is a condition involved in praying with faith:

> ***"And whenever you stand praying, if you have anything against anyone, forgive him, that your Father in heaven may also forgive you your trespasses. But if you do not forgive, neither will your Father in heaven forgive your trespasses."***
>
> **Mark 11:25-26**

Jesus says that our forgiveness of others is not only the key to an effective life of faith, but that it's also how God forgives us! Consequently, when we have unresolved sin in our lives, our faith and prayer life is very limited. How do we receive forgiveness and thus have our faith active? By forgiving those who have harmed us.

With *complete* forgiveness.

## UNFORGIVENESS GRIEVES THE HOLY SPIRIT

Ephesians 4:30 instructs us not to grieve the Holy Spirit. The word "grieve" simply means "to bring injury to someone; to wound someone." Most Christians would never dream of bringing harm to the Holy Spirit; and, in reality, they don't even know how such a thing could be possible. The Apostle Paul explains just how it happens:

> ***"Let all bitterness, wrath, anger, clamor, and evil speaking be put away from you, with all malice. And be kind to one another, tenderhearted, forgiving one another, even as God in Christ forgave you."***
>
> **Ephesians 4:31-32**

Go back to the story of Ahithophel. It is apparent that he grieved the Holy Spirit and lost his fellowship with God. God's anointing on his life was dissipating, and the most dangerous part was that he didn't even recognize it! Everyone around him—his children, family, and fellow workers—could probably see it, but Ahithophel's heart had grown so cold that he lost his spiritual perception. Why? All because of his unforgiveness and anger towards David.

The Holy Spirit is our comforter, our teacher, our guide, our revealer, and the seal of our lives until our day of redemption! He's the one who empowers us to witness and do great things for God. He is our lifeline to God, the Father! We constantly need to be asking ourselves: "Is this unforgiveness really worth bringing harm to the Holy Spirit? Is it worth short-changing all He wants to do in my life?" I believe the answer will be easy to see.

"No, it is not!"

## UNFORGIVENESS HINDERS OUR LOVE WALK

In Luke 6:29, Jesus tells us how to treat those who hurt us and subsequently become our enemies. He says that we should be willing to turn the other cheek. If they ask for your shirt, give them your coat, as well! In Matthew 5:41, Jesus teaches that if your enemies make you go one mile, then go two with them. He then adds:

> ***"But I say to you, love your enemies, bless those who curse you, do good to those who hate you, and pray for those who spitefully use you and persecute you."***
>
> **Matthew 5:44**

When I finally began to realize just how unforgiveness was affecting my love walk, I was impressed to perform a tangible act of forgiveness. I ordered an entire case of *Spirit-Filled Life* Bibles and sent them to everyone I suspected of having any ill will towards me. I also enclosed a letter that

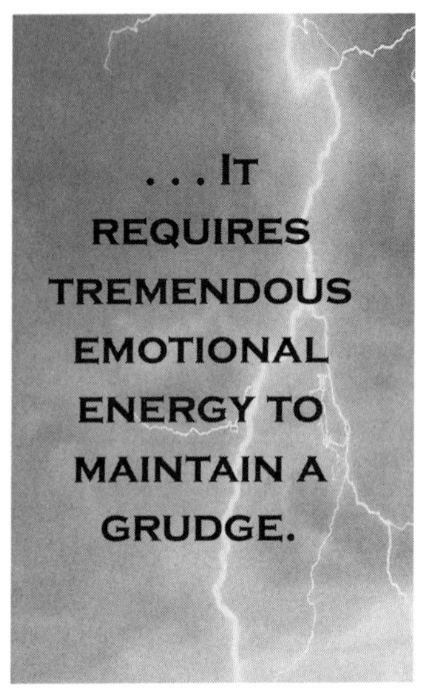


said, "I want to bless you with this Bible in Jesus' name. I'm praying for you." Isn't this obedience to the command of Jesus to bless, love, do good, and pray for your enemies?

I know this gesture did me a lot of good. It always brings blessing when we obey God's Word! But, it wasn't until I learned how to forgive completely (and not just send Bibles!) that my love walk towards everyone became truly effective.

## UNFORGIVENESS TRIGGERS OTHER DARK EMOTIONS

Friend, let me tell you that it requires tremendous emotional energy to maintain a grudge. And the process involves more than unforgiveness. Despair, bitterness, anxiety, resentment, rage, and depression are all part of the system. Depression comes when emotional energy is exhausted. Bitterness and resentment create a negative force towards the ones who hurt us. Then, as we focus on their actions (even if it happened years ago), we begin to possess the same attitude which caused our hurt in the first place. Before we know it, we become just like the people who hurt us! I believe that's exactly what happened to Ahithophel.

All of these feelings are part of what the Bible calls spiritual warfare. In Ephesians chapter six, Paul writes about the whole armor of God; but in chapters four through six, he focuses on the origin of spiritual warfare. *It begins in relationships*! In these chapters, Paul writes about relationships within the Body of Christ. His primary concern is relationships between husbands and wives and between parents and children. What do relationships have to do with spiritual warfare? The answer is that conflict in our relationships releases

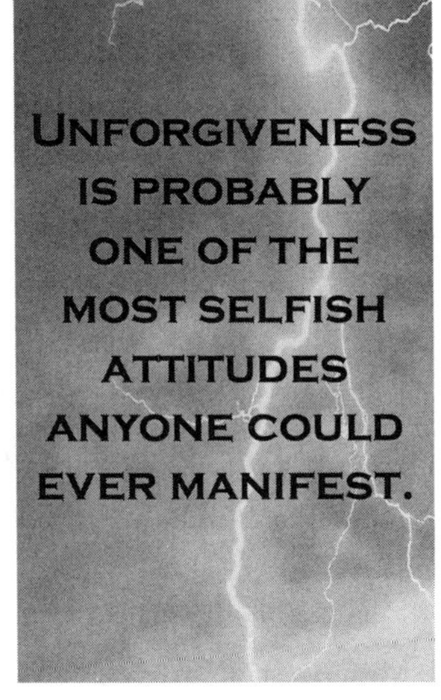

negative emotions, with unforgiveness being the paramount one.

According to the Bible, the devil's job is to steal, kill, and destroy (John 10:10). What better way for the devil to accomplish such evil than through our relationships? Conflict in relationships can breed frustration towards everyone and every situation around us. Satan knows that if we get stuck in this area, our effectiveness for the Kingdom of God will be severely limited.

## IS IT WORTH IT?

Unforgiveness is probably one of the most selfish attitudes anyone could ever manifest. When you take time to examine it openly and honestly, you will find that it's all about us! Our hurt. Our pain. Our disappointment. Our self-pity. Unforgiveness brings a false sense of revenge and healing. We *think* we are okay; but, in reality, we are dying inside.

Take a minute and look at the big picture. Consider all the other important things that are being affected—your faith, your relationship with the Holy Spirit, your love walk, your emotions, your relationships, and your family. What debilitating effect is unforgiveness having on these and other aspects of your life? Make a list. Take inventory. And then ask yourself, "Is it worth it? Is it worth jeopardizing my relationship with God? My family? My ministry? My anointing?" I believe you will see the truth . . .

. . . And the truth will set you free!

## DISCUSSION QUESTIONS

1. Read Mark 11:25-26 and identify the ways that a failure to forgive others hinders our faith in God.

2. Ephesians 4:31-32 says that not forgiving others causes the Holy Spirit to be grieved (or injured and wounded). Why do you not want to grieve the Holy Spirit?

3. Describe the emotional energy that is required to maintain a grudge.

   (a) What other dark emotions are triggered by the failure to forgive?

4. Describe the temporary and false sense of satisfaction that unforgiveness creates.

   (a) Why is this satisfaction only temporary?

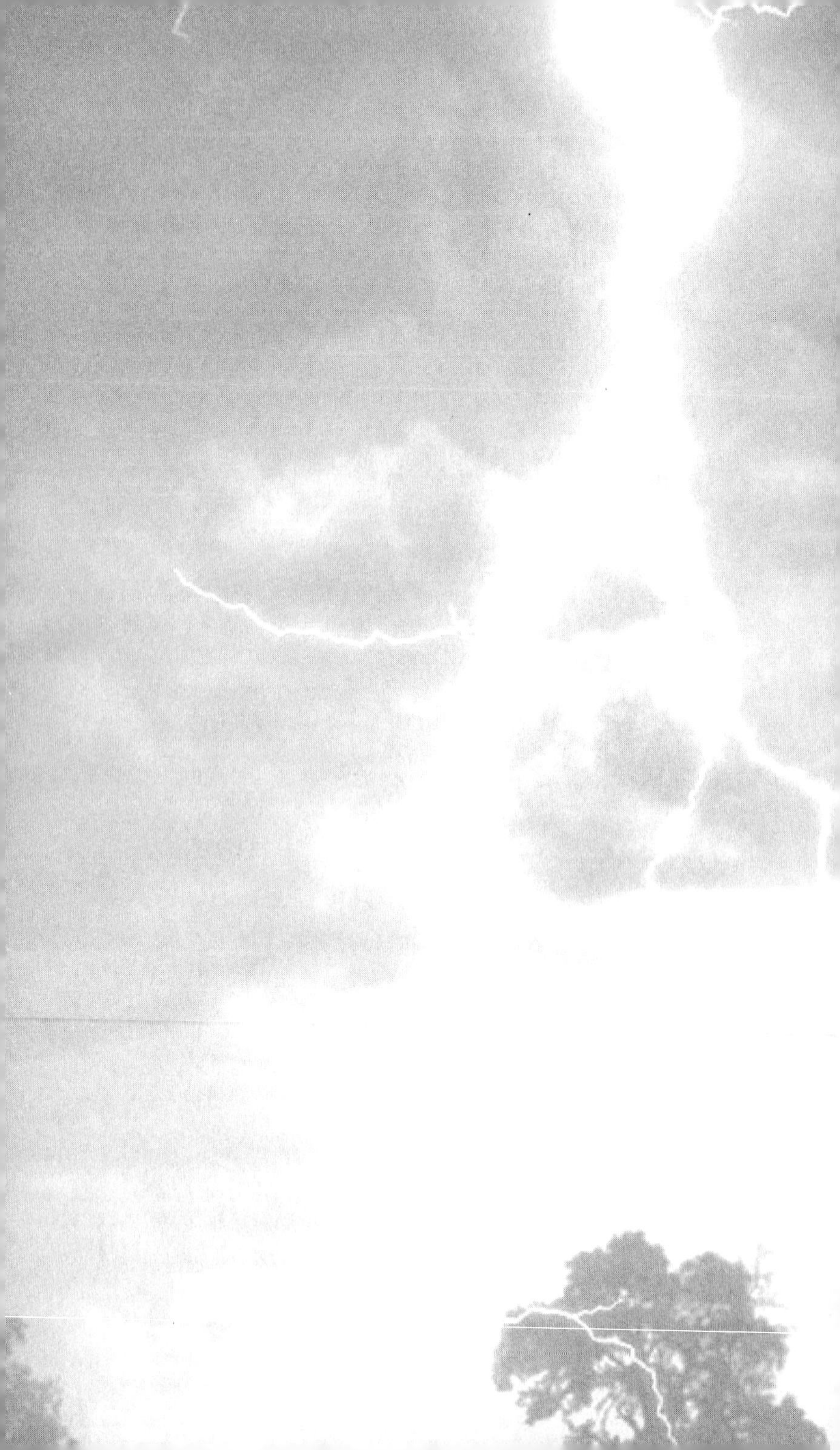

# THE ROOT OF BITTERNESS

While vacationing in the southwestern United States, my good friend Robert Morgan bit into a wild melon. He describes it as the most bitter food he has ever tried to eat! It took a long time to get the disagreeable taste out of his mouth. When you drink or eat something that is bitter, it produces an unpleasant and sharp taste. You can't wait to get rid of it and then try and wash the aftertaste away with something else. If you don't believe me, just try drinking something that has a strong and unpleasant taste.

Just like Jesus did.

While He hung on the cross, Jesus was losing

bodily fluids at a rapid pace. The Bible says He became thirsty and asked for something to drink. The Roman soldiers offered Him some of their "home brew,"—a bitter moonshine-like concoction, much like vinegar mixed with beer. When Jesus tasted it, He spit it out. He hardly let it touch His lips, and it never entered into His body (Matthew 27:34).

So, the question we need to ask ourselves is: "Why are we so quick to remove bitterness from our mouths, but we keep it in our hearts?" Just like Jesus, we have the ability to reject it and never let it get past our mouths. Yet, so many times, we drink the cup of bitterness and offense, even though it leaves a horrible taste in our souls. And, when it's digested into our system, it becomes lethal.

## BEFORE THE SUN GOES DOWN

Look at Ahithophel. Why did he take his life? Because anger, pain, and hatred had filled his soul. Bitterness had poisoned his mind and his emotions. Day after day, year after year, he rehearsed what King David had done to his family. Every day, it was like drinking radioactive water that burned every pore of his body.

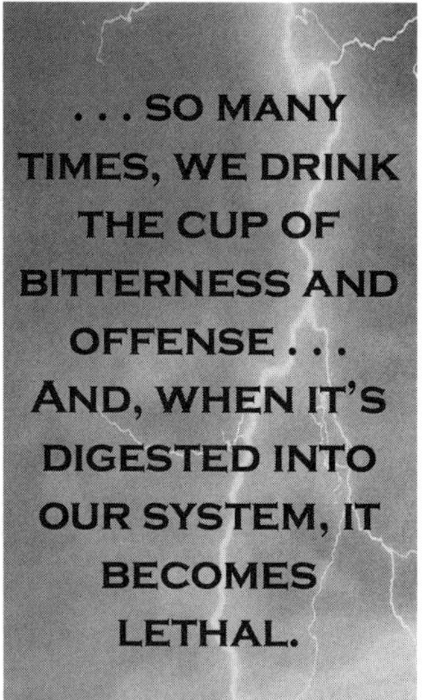


Everyone is going to get angry at something or someone. That's inevitable. But remember what Ephesians 4:26 says? We can be angry, but still not sin. You might ask yourself, "How is that possible?" The answer lies at the end of that very same verse:

> ***". . . do not let the sun go down on your wrath."***
>
> **Ephesians 4:26**

Here's the key to keep anger from turning into sin: *don't let it stay in your life more than a day!* Paul clearly states that before the sun goes down each day, you are to deal with your anger by repenting and removing it from your life. Why? Because the longer unresolved anger stays in your heart, the more it will pollute and poison your soul. And the more it pollutes your soul, the more it will poison others.

## ANGER CAN FEEL GOOD

If we are honest, we will admit that sometimes anger feels good! I remember one day my wife, Kathy, came home from the store and I could tell she was upset. I asked her what had happened and she told me that a huge stranger had yelled at her in the checkout line. Actually, he raised his voice so loudly that everyone around heard the commotion. Kathy was brought to tears right there in the store.

Immediately, the protector in me rose up! Believe me, my first reaction was *not*, "We need to pray for this man!" No, it was more like, "Where is this guy? He's not going to verbally abuse and humiliate my wife like this and get away with it! Let me at him!" The bottom line was, I was angry. But, I learned not to let it turn to sin.

What if I had let my anger towards this man (whom I have never even seen) begin to fester in me? Day after day, meditating on Kathy's experience, and imagining the incident and getting angry all over again? My *anger* would have turned into unfulfilled revenge, and that's when anger turns into sin! When anger stays in your soul for a day, a month, a year, or even longer; it becomes a big flashing amber light sending a message: "Danger! Danger! Danger!"

## THE ROOT

The Bible says that we should pursue peace with everybody. Now let's face it, living in peace is easy to do when people are behaving correctly. But when Goliath is screaming at your wife in the grocery store, it's a totally different story! The issue is that we must not stay stuck in our anger. If we do, it is a clear sign that we have missed the grace of God and there is something else brewing in our heart. The Bible says it like this:

***"Looking carefully lest anyone fall short of the grace of God; lest any root of bitterness springing up cause trouble, and by this many become defiled."***

**Hebrews 12:15**

Unresolved anger turns into bitterness over time. Then, the unfulfilled revenge or bitterness takes root in our souls. We then begin to manifest vengeful emotions towards those around us. It's the *danger of anger!*

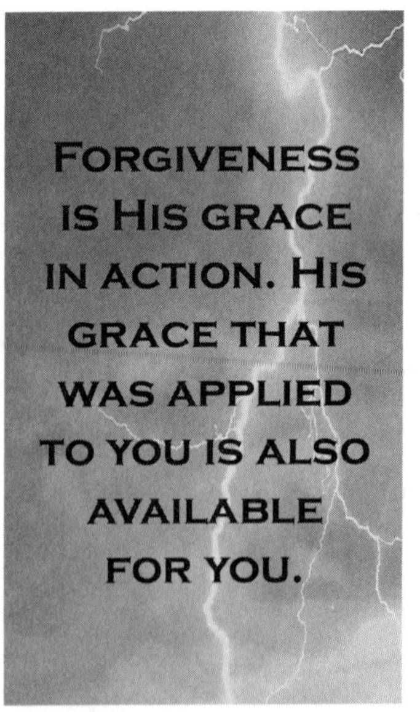


I have a minister friend who told me about one lady for whom he prayed during a church service. She came down front and was visibly upset. When he asked her what was wrong, she replied, "I can't believe he did that to me!" In talking with her for a few minutes, the pastor learned that the woman's father had molested her when she was a young girl. Then she said that her father had been dead for over 10 years. My friend looked at her and said, "Ma'am, I'm so sorry for your hurt. Certainly, this horrible thing should have never happened; but how much longer are you going to let your father rule *your* life from *his* grave?" His response shocked her, but the lights came on inside! It was a revelation that her anger had turned to deep-rooted bitterness, and the only person it was affecting was . . . her!

This same thing happens to many people. How many times have you found yourself reflecting and meditating on things that left you feeling humiliated, disrespected, or abused? Maybe it was last week or 30 years ago? Then, that anger starts welling up on the inside. Let me emphatically tell you, that anger is the "danger" signal that you need to heed!

In all of my years in the ministry, I don't think I have met many people who intentionally nursed bitterness towards others. However, I have known hundreds of people who have allowed their anger to grow until they were literally dominated by bitterness. And they didn't even realize it! The apostle Paul wrote that some of the Corinthian Christians had died because they held on to the root of bitterness

(1 Corinthians 11:30). Now, obviously you haven't died physically, but the root of bitterness will eventually bring death to your spiritual life and emotions and will damage your relationships.

But there is good news!

You don't have to live with the root of bitterness any longer. The Bible says that God's grace is sufficient for all situations, and in your weakness His power is made strong. That's good news! God's grace is not only for your sins; it is also available for you to apply to your hurts, and by faith you can extend God's grace to those who have wronged you. Just think about how much God has forgiven you. Forgiveness is His grace in action. His grace that was applied *to* you is also available *for* you.

**WHEN WE . . . APPLY GOD'S GRACE TO OUR OWN HEARTS AND TO OTHERS, ANGER CANNOT STAY IN OUR HEARTS AND GROW INTO A ROOT OF BITTERNESS.**

True forgiveness is the key! Jesus said that we should not forgive those who have harmed us seven times, but "seventy times seven!" (Matthew 18:22). That's a lot! That is 490 times . . . every day! Why? Because *His grace is sufficient!* How? By *His sufficient grace!* When we constantly apply God's grace to our own hearts and others, anger cannot stay in our hearts and grow into a root of bitterness. If it does, there is only one way to remove that root . . .

. . . By swinging the axe of forgiveness!

## DISCUSSION QUESTIONS

1. Why are we quick to remove bitterness from our taste buds, but keep it in our hearts?

2. In light of Ephesians 4:26 telling us to not allow the sun to go down on our anger, what must we do every day?

3. Have you ever known someone whose anger eventually turned into bitterness?

    (a) What other vengeful emotions did this person manifest?

4. In Matthew 18:22, how many times a day did Jesus say that we are to forgive those who sin against us?

5. Why can forgiveness be hard work?

# WARNING SIGNS

I would love to say that I recognized those danger signs in my own life; but for many years, I did not. At least once a week, I found myself reliving situations where someone had brought pain into my life. The more I thought about it, the angrier I became. And the angrier I became, the more bitterness was taking root in my heart. Out of my own hurt and pain, many times I opened my soul to other vengeful emotions. I had a hunch that I was not alone . . .

. . . Ahithophel probably did the exact same thing!

Out of his deep offense, Ahithophel opened the

door to depression, violent thoughts, and sullenness. A sullen person is somebody who shows hostility by refusing to talk or be cooperative. (If you have ever given anyone the "silent treatment," then you've been sullen!) It's a vengeful emotion and is nothing short of defiance. *It is also one of the major warning signs that anger is taking root.* But there were other signs, as well.

It is probable that Ahithophel began to be hateful, critical, and judgmental of others. Perhaps his anger turned to hostility and belligerence. Soon, he was ready to start a fight at a moment's notice, to the point of having murderous thoughts toward the one who betrayed him. Eventually, his rage cost him his life. And Ahithophel is not alone! Today, many people deal with these and similar emotions, without even recognizing that they are warning signs.

But there are more.

## VENGEANCE IS MINE!

I dealt with many of these same emotions myself. But my struggle was another step which brought me to the realization that something in my life was wrong, and that I needed to give attention to it. After pondering and brooding on what others had done to me, I would imagine ways to get even with the ones who caused the pain! I thought, "Vengeance is mine, because I have been hurt so bad!" Then, I'd snap out of it and ask myself, "Teryl, what in the world are you doing? Have you lost your mind?" All I knew to do was to ask God to forgive me for my vain imaginations, and then speak aloud words of forgiveness to those who had hurt me. But I still had no victory, and I seemed to be repeating an incessant cycle.

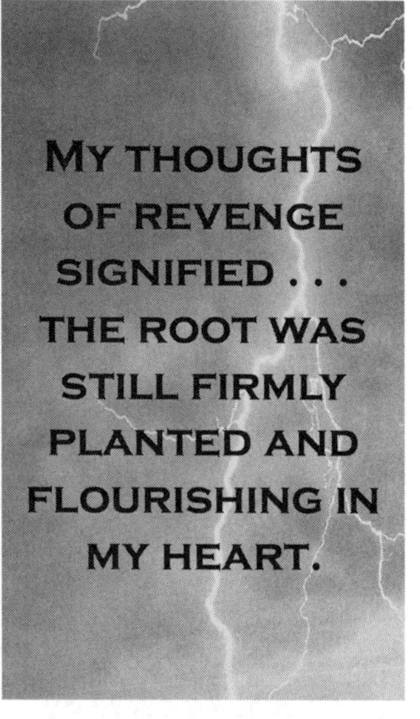


What I had failed to realize was that I had not *fully* forgiven the ones responsible for my misery. My thoughts of revenge signified that, even though I had spoken words of forgiveness, the root was still firmly planted and flourishing in my heart. As I continued to repeat the cycle of contemplating revenge and then pronouncing forgiveness, frustration and pain kept building inside me. The failure to forgive to the fullest extent allowed the devil to gain a foothold in my soul—one that I never dreamed was possible.

## THE JUDGE AND JURY

Although all of the warning signs are dangerous, there is one that is particularly ominous. It's the conviction that we are the judge and the jury to those who have harmed us. The Bible seems to indicate that Ahithophel assumed that attitude in relation to King David. In essence, he said, "God, move over. I'm going to take Your place and do Your job! I'm taking matters in my own hands!" But, the reality was that

WHEN WE BECOME THE SELF-APPOINTED JUDGE, JURY, AND IN SOME SITUATIONS THE EXECUTIONER, WE HAVE ENTERED A DANGER ZONE!

Ahithophel didn't have to act as judge. God had already sent the prophet, Nathan, to confront David with his sin, and David had already repented in sackcloth and ashes. God had already forgiven him of his sin, even though David would reap some terrible consequences for his actions.

But, Ahithiophel just couldn't let go of his lust for revenge.

Friend, there is only one righteous judge—God. The Bible says that Jesus is a High Priest who understands our weaknesses, for He faced all the same tests that we experience. In other words, He knows your pain, your hurt, and your betrayal. Jesus understands the businessman who has been swindled out of a pile of money. He feels the sting of rejection and failure when your spouse informs you that the marriage is over and walks out. Jesus feels the pain. He knows the agony. He feels what you feel. His ears are not deaf, and His eyes are not closed to your situation.

The trouble begins when we adopt the Ahithophel approach and say. "God, I can take care of this." When we become the self-appointed judge, jury, and in some situations the executioner, we have entered a danger zone! The Bible clearly says that when we presume to be the judge, we set ourselves up to judged—by God Himself (Matthew 7:1).

## THE RIGHT WAY

Maybe no one can understand all of the pain you have lived through. I thought the same thing. But, you are never alone, because of the undeniable truth that *God knows exactly what you feel*! He alone is the judge. God knows how to clear your name. He knows how to fight your battles. He knows how to bind up your wounds and heal your broken heart. The Bible says that He even goes so far as to prepare a table for you in the presence of your enemies (Psalms 23:5)! It also says in the Word that He will turn your enemies into a footstool (Psalms 110:1).

God knows how to settle your wrongs and balance the scales.

> ***"Vengeance is mine, I will repay, saith the Lord."***
>
> **Romans 12:19 (KJV)**

You have to heed the warning signs and yield to God's grace. God will take care of the rest!

## DISCUSSION QUESTIONS

1. Have you ever found yourself reliving situations from the past, where someone brought pain into your life?

   (a) How frequently does this happen?

2. Why does brooding about emotional pain from the past open the door to depression, violent thoughts, and sullenness (refusing to talk or be cooperative with others)?

   (a) Why can it also trigger hate, belligerence, and a critical attitude?

3. What is wrong with our being the judge and jury and wanting to execute judgment on those who have hurt us?

(a) Why does Matthew 7:1 say that this attitude sets us up to be judged by God Himself?

4. Do you struggle with inward thoughts of revenge?

(a) Is a root of bitterness flourishing in your heart?

# A STRONGER FORCE

My time spent with my counselor was not fun! Actually, it was very painful at times—painful in the sense that I had to go back and deal with some hurts and bruises from the past. What I did find out during that time was how many hurts and pains I had just stuffed deep down inside me. I had convinced myself that they would somehow just disappear. But they never did.

By nature, I'm the type who always has an answer. No matter what the situation, I can always figure something out, make it work, come up with a solution, and keep right on rolling. I guess you could say I was a "never let them see you sweat" type of person. For years, this attitude worked just fine!

But, when it came to my anger, I was miserably failing. More than just failing, I was dying on the inside.

One day, my counselor helped me to see something I had never seen before. I remember him telling me, "Teryl, you have a weakness; but it's okay to be weak." "What?" I replied. "Weak? Are you kidding me? I'm not a weak person!" About that time, I was ready to jump on the table, flex my muscles, and quote every "I am strong" scripture I could possibly remember! But the truth was, he was right . . . on both accounts.

I had a weakness.

But it was okay!

## THE WEAK

The revelation finally came to me that I didn't have it all together. I didn't have all the answers this time. In fact, there were far more questions than solutions. That's when I began to ask, "Lord, what do You think about all of this? What's Your answer for my anger?" And I remember hearing the words of the Apostle Paul:

***"And He said to me, 'My grace is sufficient for you, for My strength is made perfect in weakness.' Therefore most gladly I will rather boast in my infirmities, that the power of Christ may rest upon me."***

**2 Corinthians 12:9**

Even though I had quoted and preached on this verse countless times, it finally hit home in my heart. I started to see that God was not attracted to my strengths! Heaven doesn't need all my abilities! According to this verse, God is attracted to *weakness*. Why? Because it is in our weakness—when we don't have all the answers—that God's strength becomes the perfect solution. I came to realize that God is looking for the person who can say, "Lord, through You I can do all things; but apart from You, I can do nothing!"

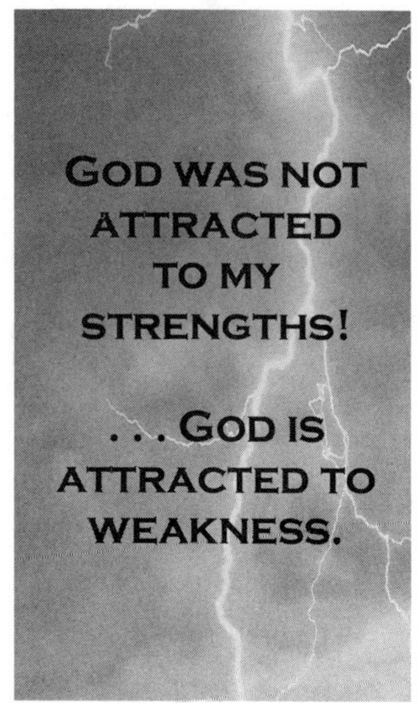

WHEN I BEGAN TO UNDERSTAND THE FORCE THAT IS MORE POWERFUL THAN ANGER . . . MY JOURNEY OF HEALING BEGAN.

At this time, I began to cry out, "*God, I'm weak. Without You, God, I'm helpless! I ask You to help me learn how to grieve over these hurts and these pains. God, help me mourn these losses and all of the rejection, relational confusion, disappointment, and despair. God, I pray that You would heal my heart. I know your grace is sufficient for me. Lord, I need Your grace.*"

## GOD'S GRACE

For about three months, every night that I wasn't busy at the church, I sat on our back porch and prayed this prayer:

> *"Lord, I know Your grace is the unmerited favor that You give us freely through Christ. I know Your grace isn't based on my performance. And I also know that I can only receive*

> *Your grace by faith. God, Your grace is sufficient for me. Give me the grace to mourn. By faith, I receive the grace to get this poison out of my heart! Lord Jesus, I know that Your grace is sufficient for me!"*

Then, I began to meditate on His grace. Big tears would often flow down my cheeks as the Holy Spirit gently emptied my heart and emotions of the pent-up pain.

The most ironic thing was that all my life I had been a Pentecostal/Charismatic Christian. Of course, the word "charisma" comes from the Greek word "charis," which means "grace." I knew how to put faith in God's grace for salvation and healing. I knew that the grace of God could move mountains, so why wasn't the mountain inside me moving? The reason was that I was trying to move it all by myself.

When I began to understand the force that is more powerful than anger—*God's grace*—my journey of healing began. God took me back to all of those hurts and difficult places in order that I might release them to His grace! Honestly, I felt the weakest I have ever felt in my life; but at the same time, I felt the strongest. I had to rely completely on Him. Daily, I would pray, "Lord, by faith I receive Your abundant grace. I fully forgive every person who has ever hurt me. I release them to your grace today."

## FIRST STEPS

Friend, if you are filled with anger, you cannot receive deliverance without the grace of God. Of course, harboring that anger feels good in the beginning! It seems to be our "right" to be mad; and in some way, anger brings a certain satisfaction. But, no matter how good it might feel, at some point that anger will turn to bitterness and unfulfilled revenge. Then, it's a toxic poison brewing inside of you *and* coming out of you toward others.

It's time to get real with God. I had to. Was it easy? No. Did it challenge me to the core of my soul? Yes! And it will do the same for you. But it is at that point that God's grace can completely take over and begin the healing process. Why don't you start by saying:

*"Lord, I'm hurting! I'm full of anger and I want to be free. Free to live. Free to love. Free to be me again. Come and heal my heart, bind-up my brokenness. I forgive those who have hurt me, and I cancel the debt they owe. I extend grace to others, and I receive Your grace for me! Your grace to heal me where I am hurting. Lord, I receive Your mercy!"*

Congratulations! You are on your way to freedom!

## DISCUSSION QUESTIONS

1. Why according to 2 Corinthians 12:9 do our strengths and abilities keep us from God's grace?

    (a) Why is God's grace only activated by faith? (See Ephesians 2:8.)

2. Describe a time that you were blind to your need for God's grace.

3. In what way is God's grace sufficient for you?

# BREAK THE CHAINS

I've known people who have been enslaved to anger for so long that they actually forgot what triggered their wrath and resentment! They can't remember the person or circumstances that launched them down the road of rage. It's ironic isn't it? Often the person who hurt us isn't even aware that we are suffering. But when I hold on to an offense, I make myself a prisoner who can't escape the tyranny of what another has said or done.

Maybe you're angry with God! Many people are. Maybe you are blaming Him for the death of a child, the loss of a career, or the break-up of a marriage. It really isn't His fault. He loves you! For your sake, you need to forgive Him!

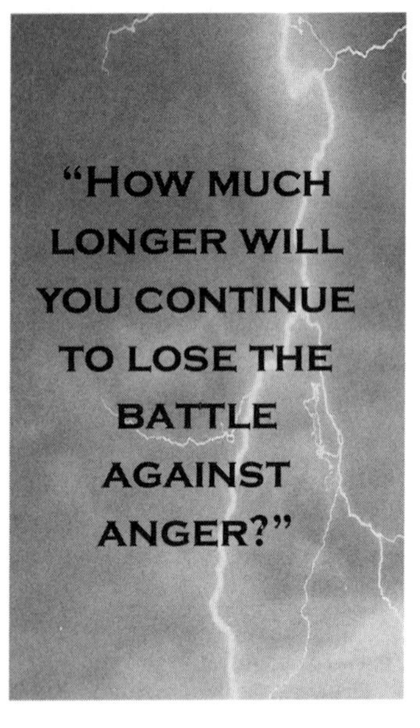


You might be angry with yourself. There are countless numbers of people who don't believe they can ever forgive themselves for things they have done. The healthiest thing you can do is to repent and ask God to forgive you, and then forgive yourself. Do three things: turn away from your sin, turn towards Christ, and then let yourself off the hook!

Take a moment and look around you. Is anger negatively affecting your relationships? Your marriage? Your children? Your career? Your spiritual walk with the Lord? Is the "kiss of death" still penetrating your soul? Have you gotten to the place where you don't trust anyone? Are the walls you have built around yourself actually *protecting* you, or are they *isolating* you from others? These are hard questions to face. I know. I had to face each of them . . . and more.

If you see yourself in any of these situations, then the next question is, “How much longer will you continue to lose the battle against anger?” That, too, is a hard question to face. But, Friend, it is one you will have to come to grips with. Just like I did. And when I did, I knew I had to change.

And so can you!

## TODAY IS THE DAY

There’s an old adage that says, “Today is the first day of the rest of your life.” It’s a true proverb. Every time the sun comes up, it’s a new day. It is, indeed, the first day of the remainder of your life. But, there is something else that happens every time a new sunrise breaks the horizon. The Bible says that God’s mercies and compassions are *new every morning* (Lamentations 3:22-23). That simply means that every day there is a brand new dimension of God’s grace—directed towards you.

A new day of forgiveness.

A new way to show compassion.

A new day for God’s grace to heal.

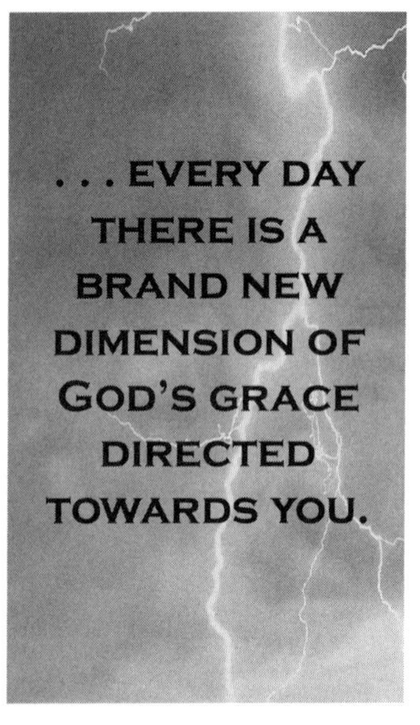


My friend, don't be the one who says, "Oh, I can forgive another day. I handle things differently than others." Let me assure you that is a deception from the enemy. Sure, it might make you feel good to hang on to your anger for another day, but the time will come when you don't have another day! You won't have another opportunity. It will, in fact, be too late.

The Bible says that *today* is the day of salvation; *now* is the right time! (2 Corinthians 6:2) Is it easy to be the first one to ask for forgiveness? No, it isn't! Is it easy to wrestle with hurts and pains from the past? No, it isn't! Is it easy to pardon the payment owed by those who have hurt you? No, it isn't! It takes courage. It takes faith. It takes the grace of God in action. But it is necessary if you want to live a life free of anger and frustration.

## GOD KNOWS

Always remember that God knows every single difficulty you have endured. The divorce. The betrayal. The loss of income. The false accusations. The harsh words spoken behind your back. He knows it all. And none of it took Him by surprise or took Him off His throne. *He is still God*!

When it felt like God was a million miles away, He was right there with you. He felt every heartache, knew every situation, and captured every tear you shed. Remember the promise that He declared to you:

***"I will never leave you nor forsake you."***

**Hebrews 13:5**

*The Message* Bible says it like this:

*"I'll never let you down, never walk off and leave you."*

It's good news to know that God knows *everything*, and yet He has never left you!

## A DEFINING MOMENT

I believe you are about to have a defining moment in your life, just as I did. I can tell you from my own experience that it is the day you will look back on and say, "That was the day my emotional freedom began! Free from the hurts. Free from the past. Free from anger." It could be one of the best days of your entire life!

It was for me.

When you forgive, you aren't saying that what someone did to you was right, because it wasn't! When you forgive, you are not saying that you necessarily trust the person to whom you are extending forgiveness, nor are you setting yourself up to be hurt again. On the contrary, when you forgive, you are declaring that you deserve to be free from the tyranny that you experienced. You are saying that God's grace is sufficient! You are placing your trust in the All-Sufficient God to bind up your brokenness! You are manifesting the nature of God, who has forgiven you in Christ!

It's time to break the chains! To live free from the *danger of anger!*

WHEN YOU FORGIVE . . . YOU ARE MANIFESTING THE NATURE OF GOD, WHO HAS FORGIVEN YOU IN CHRIST!

If you are struggling with anger, the important thing is to identify the root issues triggering your emotions and embrace God's grace that will set you free. His grace *is* sufficient!

Let's start by praying this prayer aloud from your heart:

> *"Lord Jesus, I confess to You the anger and rage that is within my soul. I confess that I am hurting on the inside. Give me the grace to be in touch with and to mourn the pain I've experienced. Help me to grieve and even weep, and to allow pain and poison to escape my soul. I cancel my right for revenge. I tear up the notes of*

*indebtedness owed by those who have caused my suffering. I choose to release and to forgive those who have mistreated me. I forgive them in Jesus name! Though I am weak, Your grace is sufficient for me! Amen!"*

How is your relationship with God? If you aren't certain that you have trusted the shed blood of Christ as the full payment for your sin, why not pray this prayer aloud right now?

*"Lord Jesus, thank You for dying on the cross for me. Right now, I repent of my sins and trust Your shed blood as full payment for all of my sins. I believe that You are the Son of God and that God has raised You from the dead. I now receive You as my personal Savior. I commit my life unreservedly to You as my Lord. Thank You for hearing my prayer, forgiving my sins, and coming into my life as You promised. Amen."*

## DISCUSSION QUESTIONS

1. Are you angry with God? Do you hold God responsible for the death of a child?

   (a) The loss of your career?

   (b) The break-up of a marriage?

2. Why are these things not God's fault?

3. Why is it hard for people who are angry with themselves to turn away from their failure, turn to Christ, and then to let themselves off the hook?

4. Is anger negatively affecting your relationships?

   (a) Your marriage?

(b) Your children? Your career? Your walk with the Lord?

5. When you forgive, is this the same as admitting that the evil that someone did to you was all right?

6. Why is forgiving someone not the same as trusting them?

# AUTHOR'S NOTE

Do we have conclusive proof that Ahithophel was Bathsheba's grandfather? No, there is only circumstantial evidence. It could be a coincidence that Ahithophel's son and Bathsheba's father were both named Eliam. It could be a coincidence that Ahithophel just decided to turn against King David without cause, but it wasn't very likely.

Was Uriah the Hittite really a member of King David's special royal forces? Indeed, he was! Second Samuel 23:39 lists him as one of David's mighty men, along with "Eliam, the son of Ahithophel, the Gilionite," (verse 34). Another coincidence? Maybe, but maybe not.

Blessings,

Teryl Todd

# ABOUT TERYL TODD

Teryl believes that life should not be something we endure, but something we enjoy! His focus is on equipping people to be "love with skin-on for a hurting world." He often refers to himself as "a guy who is on his way to heaven, and who wants to help as many people as possible make heaven their home." He enjoys praying, working-out, riding motorcycles, and college football.

He and his wife, Kathy, have been in ministry for almost 35 years, and are in love with each other and with the Lord! They currently reside in Tallahassee, Florida, and are the parents of three grown daughters, a son-in-law, and a grandson: Terri, Kristin, Kathryn, Byron, and Braden.

He has served as Senior Pastor of Evangel Assembly of God since 2002. Previously, he and Kathy helped to plant a new congregation on the North Shore of Chicago, where they served as Senior Pastors for 14 years. Prior to that, he served Regent University (CBN) in Virginia Beach, VA, as Vice-President for Student Affairs and Chaplain. He has also served congregations in Virginia Beach, Virginia, and St. Augustine, Florida.

Teryl is a graduate of Emmanuel College (B.S.); Regent University (M.A.); and Southwestern University (M.A.).

# CONTACT

Teryl W. Todd
P. O. Box 180754
Tallahassee, FL 32318-0754

Phone

850.385.1815

Fax

850.385.4497

E-mail

orders@teryltodd.com

www.TerylTodd.com